Building the B.M.T.

36th Street to Ninth Avenue

by James Poulos

Building the B.M.T.
36th Street to Ninth Avenue
Copyright © 2016 by James Poulos

Photo credits: Collection of Alan Zelazo unless otherwise noted.
Maps and Drawings: Collection of James Poulos
BRT/BMT Standard Brochure p.15 Courtesy Bill Zucker

All rights reserved. No part of this book may be reproduced in any form by any electronic or mechanical means including photocopying, recording, or information storage and retrieval without permission in writing from the author.

ISBN-13: 978-1533021045
ISBN-10: 153302104X

Book Website
www.bmt-lines.com

INTRODUCTION

On October 27, 1904 the Interborough Rapid Transit Company (IRT) began operating New York's first subway. The system was very popular and it soon became obvious that it needed to be expanded. In 1907 the Public Service Commission was founded which took over the regulation of the electric and gas companies as well as the street railways and rapid transit companies. In 1910 the commission proposed a new subway that it called the "Tri-Borough System". This new plan incorporated the Fourth Avenue Subway in Brooklyn, a route that had been previously planned and construction was already under way since 1909. The section between Flatbush Avenue Extension, Fulton Street, Ashland Place to 43rd Street and 4th Avenue was completed pursuant to these contracts. A provision was made at 40th Street for a branch to Coney Island via New Utrecht Avenue (West End Route).

Meanwhile the City of New York was negotiating with both the Brooklyn Rapid Transit Company (BRT) and the Interborough Rapid Transit Company. The BRT controlled a vast network of surface and elevated lines in Brooklyn, while the IRT controlled the original subway route in Manhattan and had taken control of the Manhattan elevated lines. The negotiations culminated on March 19, 1913 with the signing of the Dual Contracts under which both companies would participate in the subway expansion. The BRT incorporated a subsidiary called the New York Municipal Railway (NYM) to enter into the contract with the city. The NYM was then leased back to the New York Consolidated RR, the BRT subsidiary already operating the elevated lines. The 1922 issue of Moody's Manual of Investments described the arrangement as follows:

> "Prior to the execution of the contracts with the city, and pursuant to the predetermined arrangement, the companies owning the existing railroads which are to form part of the new rapid transit system, namely the Brooklyn Union Elevated RR Co., the Canarsie RR Co, and the Sea Beach Ry Co. were duly consolidated into the New York Consolidated RR Co., and subsequently the latter company took from the New York Municipal Ry Corp. an assignment of the operating provisions of the City contracts assumed by that corporation, so that the New York Consolidated RR Co will be the operator of the new system."

While the Triborough Plan was no longer under consideration, most of its proposed routes would be incorporated into the new "Dual System". This included the 4th Avenue Subway which was to go to the BRT for operation. The BRT and the Public Service Commission agreed on a change to the routing of the West End and Culver branches. Instead of branching off at 40th Street which would require a new tunnel, they would use the existing "Culver Tunnel" at 38th Street which was already owned by the South Brooklyn Railway, the BRT's freight subsidiary. This necessitated removing the original south half of the 36th Street / 4th Avenue Station and extending the platforms to the north. The original south mezzanine was closed off, a part of which is used today as a signal relay room. At Ninth Avenue a two-level station would be built with two island platforms on each level. West End trains used the upper level as the D Route still does today. Culver subway/elevated trains and South Brooklyn freights operated through the lower level. Interlockings north of the station allowed Culver trains to operate either through the Fourth Avenue Subway or the Fifth Avenue Elevated line.

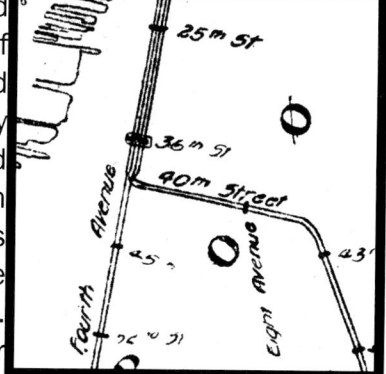

Triborough Plan of 1910

Today the lower level lies abandoned since the Culver connection to the Fourth Avenue subway was severed.

The reconstruction of the 36th Street Station began in 1914. On June 23rd, 1916 West End trains began operating through the Culver Tunnel and the Fourth Avenue Subway. The track/electrical map on the next page shows the complex track arrangement, followed by artist renderings of the site on pages 7 and 8. The BRT documented virtually every step of its construction. What follows in this book are photographs taken by the staff photographers of the BRT documenting the "remodeling" of the 36th Street Station and the extension of the line via 38th Street to Ninth Avenue. The photographs are in chronological sequence from October 1914 through December 1915.

On November 1, 1918 the BRT was hit with a wildcat strike. Managers and other non-union personnel were put to work operating trains regardless of how little operating experience they had. One such "replacement" motorman was behind schedule as he was speeding a Brighton Beach bound train down what is today the Franklin Avenue shuttle. The train derailed on a curve and hit a tunnel wall on the approach to the Prospect Park Station. In what is still the greatest tragedy in NYC Transit history 93 people lost their lives. The repercussions of this disaster combined with other factors related to cost overruns and delays in the completion of the city contract pushed the BRT into bankruptcy.

In 1923 the BRT was reorganized as the Brooklyn Manhattan Transit Corporation (BMT). The BMT's new leadership promptly sought to improve service and its public image. It became arguably one of the most profitable, innovative and progressive transit operators of its time. In its final year of operation, 1939, the BMT would introduce to the public an aluminum subway car that included such amenities as mirrors and mohair upholstered seats. Rubber springs and rubber-sandwiched wheels helped mitigate noise and an air filtration system improved interior air quality. Unfortunately political and financial constraints forced the company to sell its operations to the City of New York in 1940. The city cancelled contracts for the innovations the BMT was offering in favor of returning to older, standardized technology. Only today is the MTA considering open gangway cars, a style the BMT championed back in 1923. We will never know how far ahead we would be today in terms of technology and comfort had the BMT remained in business.

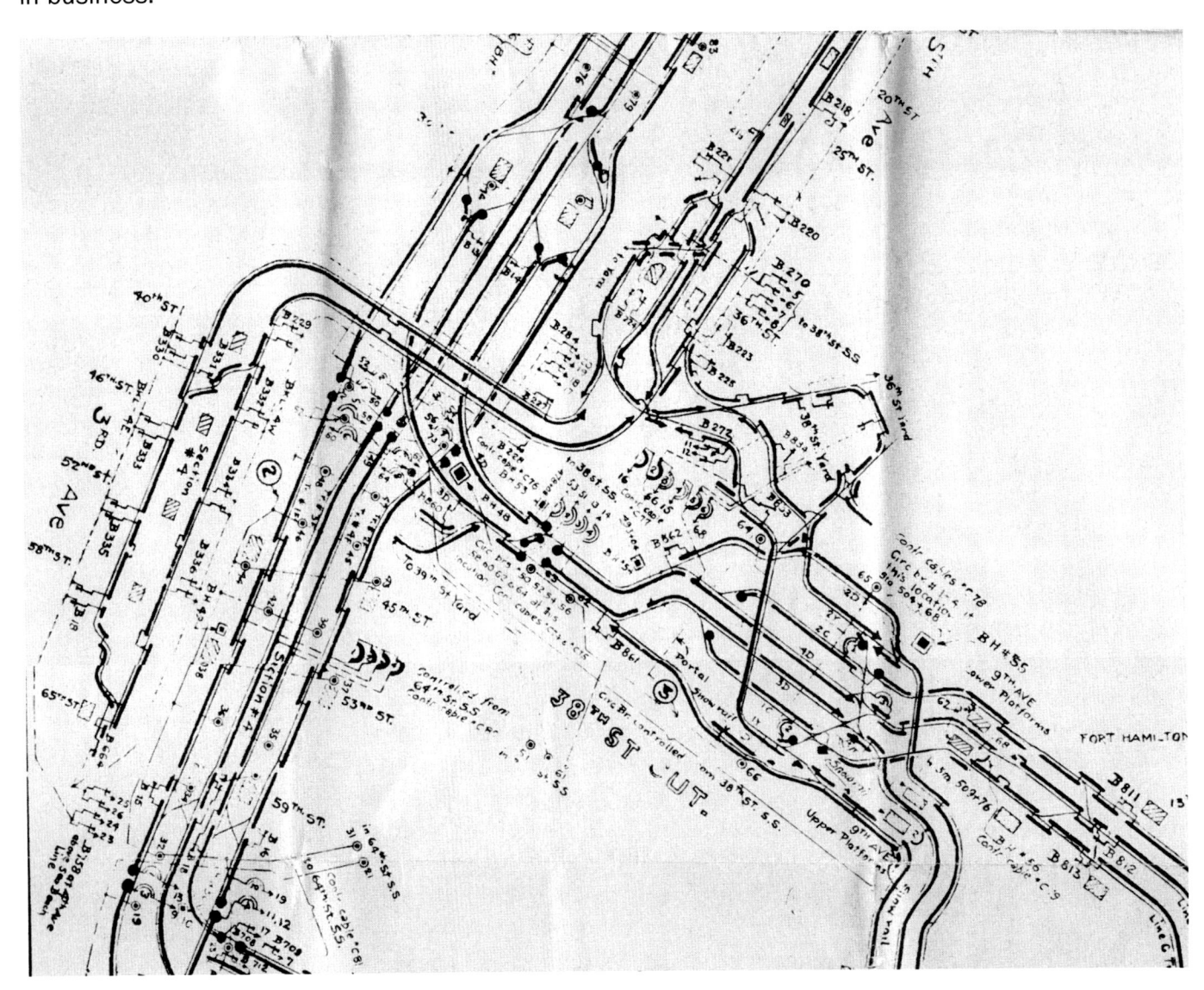

PUBLIC SERVICE COMMISSION REPORTS

The following are exerpts from the Public Service Commission Reports with respect to the construction of this route which was designated "Route No. 39, Section No. 1":

1914 p.199: This section covers the turnout from the Fourth Avenue subway near 38th street and extends to about Tenth avenue and 38th street. The tracks are in subway, open-cut and on elevated structure, and with other Brooklyn Rapid Transit tracks pass through private property between 37th and 38th streets. Elaborate plans are made for this locality for the interchange of traffic between the various lines and a large yard is to be provided. On account of difficulty of separating this work of changes to the Brooklyn Rapid Transit lines from that for the City-built lines, Modifying Agreement No. 1, of Contract No. 4, was executed to permit the New York Municipal Railway Corporation to do the reconstruction work of the Fourth Avenue line from 33d street and Fourth avenue for this connection and of the lines to Tenth avenue.

Construction drawings were completed for the reconstruction of the Fourth Avenue subway between 33d street and 38th street, including plans for the refabrication of old material. Drawings prepared by Jacobs & Davies, Inc., consulting engineers for the New York Municipal Railway Corporation, for work on 38th street between Fourth avenue and Tenth avenue, were approved. The alignment of this line was moved north about forty feet. Estimates were made of the saving due to the shifting of the line east of Seventh avenue.

1914 p.204: Work on this section was begun on February 3, 1914, by the New York Municipal Railway Corporation under direct charge of Messrs. Jacobs & Davies, consulting engineers. It is being executed on a force account basis and will cost approximately $1,800,000. It includes the reconstruction of the 36th Street station of the Fourth Avenue subway, the construction of a turnout into the Culver cut at 38th street, and the reconstruction of the Culver cut between Fourth and Tenth avenues, part of which will be a subway and part an open cut. The Fourth avenue portion is a four-track subway.

Excavation and the work of demolishing the old concrete on Fourth avenue is complete and the reconstruction well under way. The retaining walls between Fourth and Fifth avenues are completed. The excavation between Fifth and Tenth avenues was made by two 70-ton steam shovels. The spoil was removed by standard gauge locomotives and dump cars and was used to fill in the Dycker meadows south of 86th street. About 57 per cent of the estimated value of the work is completed. The following tabulation gives the work done under the principal items of construction, from the commencement of work on this section to December 31, 1914, and the total estimated value of work completed during the same period:

> Excavation above M. H. W. . . . . 171,810 cu. yds.
> Concrete . . . . 14,375 cu. yds.
> Steel delivered . . . . 2,100 tons
> Steel erected . . . . 338 tons .
> Waterproofing ply . . . . 29 sq. yds.
> Brick and mastic . . . . 4 cu. yds.
> Ducts, 4-way . . . . 9,500 lin. ft.
> Underpinning buildings . . . . 40 lin. ft.
> Total value of work completed, as estimated, $1,026,000.

1914 p. 206: Sewer work on this section when under way will involve the construction of 2,178 linear feet of new sewers, including 659 feet of 24-inch off-line sewer in 38th street.

1915 p. 245: This is a three track extension of the Fourth Avenue subway, from about 38th street to Coney Island. It extends easterly in a cut between 37th and 39th streets to a point near 10th avenue, where the tracks ascend to an elevated structure, extending thence over 10th avenue and New Utrecht avenue to 81st street, over private property to 86th street, and thence over 86th street and Stillwell avenue to a connection at Avenue Y with the New York Municipal tracks to Coney Island. This is known as Route No. 39, and is divided into two sections, Nos. 1 and 2. A connection is provided on this line for the Gravesend Avenue line.

Route No. 39 Section No. 1 – The connection for this line from the Fourth Avenue subway was shifted from 41st street at the request of the New York Municipal Railway Corporation. That has made necessary the reconstruction of a portion of the subway on Fourth avenue between 33d and 38th streets. For convenience this work is included with Route No. 39, Section No. 1. Provision is made on this section also for connection with the Gravesend Avenue line. Under the Dual Contracts, the right of way through which this section runs was turned over to the City for the construction of a rapid transit line which will replace the present service. The company proposes also to build a large yard in the vicinity and make a connection with the Fifth Avenue Elevated line. On account of the necessity of doing the work under traffic conditions and the difficulty of separating construction work, the company, in a supplemental agreement with the City, undertook to do the work of this section at cost. With the approval of the Commission, Jacobs & Davies, Inc., were made construction engineers for the work. This work was begun on February 13, 1914 and is being executed on a force account basis at a cost of about $3,000,000. Plans were completed during the year.

1915 p. 246: The reconstruction of the subway from 33d to 38th street, including the 36th Street station, is complete, and has been in operation since June 19, 1915, two of the four tracks being in use. Sidewalk restoration and paving are practically complete. The work of reconstructing the old Culver out between Fourth and Tenth avenues is complete. The Ninth Avenue station, including its superstructure, which is a one-story brick structure trimmed with terra cotta, and which has a copper roof, is practically complete, with the exception of the regrading of Ninth avenue from the station buildings to 39th street. Operation has not yet begun in the cut, although the tracks have been placed and ballasted throughout. About 99 per cent of the contract value of the work has been performed.

1915 p. 248: The following summary gives the progress of work during the year on contracts let for station finish, track installation, and other work enumerated, in connection with the New Utrecht Avenue Line, Route No. 39, Sections Nos. 1 and 2, respectively:

Route No. 39, Section No. 1, Ninth Avenue Station Superstructure.— This is a one-story brick structure, trimmed with terra cotta, and having a copper roof. The Snare & Triest Company, to whom this contract was let by the New York Municipal Railway Corporation on July 8, 1915, sublet most of the work. The contract price is $23,940. Work was begun on August 6, 1914. This structure is now practically completed, with the exception of some of the interior finish.

The contract time expired on October 8, 1915. but was extended to December 15, 1915. About 99 per cent of the contract value of the work has been performed.

NINTH AVENUE
NEW UTRECHT AVE
40TH STREET
39 STREET
EIGHTH AVENUE
37TH STREET

5TH AVE.
6TH AVE.
8TH AVE.
37TH STREET
39TH STREET
NINTH AVENUE
NEW UTRECHT AVENUE

THE FOURTH AVENUE SUBWAY
[From a pamphlet issued on the opening of the line June 19, 1915]

South Brooklyn is responsible for the beginning of the agitation which resulted in the Fourth Avenue subway. That section of Brooklyn had grown so rapidly that the existing elevated railroad and surface car facilities became inadequate, and the citizens voiced a demand for better transportation service.

FIRST STEPS TAKEN IN 1905

Ten years ago the first official steps were taken to supply the deficiency, when the Board of Rapid Transit Railroad Commissioners on June 1, 1905, adopted the route for the original Fourth Avenue subway. This route was approved by the board of estimate and apportionment on July 1st of the same year. Being unable to get the necessary consents from property owners to the construction of this road. The Rapid Transit Commission applied to the Appellate Division of the Supreme Court, First Department, which, on June 18,1906, authorized its construction.

On December 7, 1906, the board of estimate and apportionment recommended that alternate bids be let: First, for construction alone, and second, for construction, equipment, and operation. On May 31, 1907 the Rapid Transit Commission requested the board of estimate to rescind the above resolution so that bids for construction alone might be asked for, and authorized the chief engineer and counsel to prepare the plans and contracts. On June 4, 1907, the board of estimate and apportionment rescinded the resolution and authorized the Commission to advertise for bids for construction only.

On June 27, 1907, the Rapid Transit Commission approved the plans and contracts except those for Section 11-A-1 covering that part of the route from Ashland place and Fulton street to Fourth avenue and Sackett street.

On July 1, 1907, the Public Service Commission succeeded the Rapid Transit Commission, and on July 30th held a public bearing upon the forms of contracts as determined upon by the Rapid Transit Commission. In October and November, 1907, the Public Service Commission approved the plans and contracts with some changes in grades and an increase in the height of the subway. The height was fixed at fifteen feet in the clear. On December 9th the Commission authorized counsel and chief engineer to prepare the contract and plans for Section 11-A-1. These were prepared and a hearing was held upon the form of contract on February 18, 1908. On March 10, 1908, the Commission approved the plans and form of contract and transmitted them to the board of estimate and apportionment. On March 27, 1908 the board of estimate and apportionment approved the form of contract and requested the Public Service Commission to advertise for bids immediately. On March 31st the Commission ordered that invitations to contractors be published as advertisements according to law. The advertisements, beginning early in April, appeared once a week for four weeks, and bids were opened by the Commission on May 8, 1908.

FIRST CONTRACTS DELAYED BY LIMIT LITIGATION

On May 22, 1908, the Commission awarded contracts for all six sections to the lowest bidder for each section, and on May 26, 1908, transmitted the awards for approval to the board of estimate and apportionment, with a requisition for $2,850,000 to start the work.

The aggregate amount of the contracts awarded was about $15,856,000, and Comptroller Metz, holding that the full amount would be charged against the debt limit if the contracts were approved, gave it as his opinion that the city had not sufficient borrowing capacity to justify it in approving the contracts. To test the question, Jefferson M. Levy brought a taxpayer's suit for an injunction to restrain the board of estimate and apportionment from approving the contracts. This injunction was served upon the board of estimate June 12, 1908, and continued in force until the latter part of October, 1909, during which time the question of the debt limit was taken up to the Court of Appeals for determination. Soon after the issuance of the injunction the Supreme Court appointed General Benjamin F. Tracy referee to investigate and determine what the city's margin under the debt limit was as of June 30, 1908. The referee spent several months in the investigation and made his report in April, 1909, holding that the margin of the city's borrowing capacity on the date in question was about $104,000,000. In arriving at this amount, he had purposely excluded contract liabilities of the city where contracts had been signed, but no payments had been made or bonds issued in payment thereon. The report of the referee was appealed to the Appellate Division, which, without going into the merits of the case, approved it pro-forma and an appeal was immediately taken to the Court of Appeals. This court handed down its decision in October, 1909. In the main it confirmed the report of the referee, but overruled him in his action excluding contract liabilities upon which no bonds had been issued or payments made, holding that the full amount of such contracts must be computed in figuring the borrowing margin under the debt limit. The decision reduced the borrowing capacity as of June 30, 1908, to about $54,000,000.

As soon as the Court of Appeals' decision was received officially by the city authorities, the injunction restraining the board of estimate and apportionment from acting upon the Fourth Avenue subway contracts was dissolved, and at the meeting on October 29, 1909, the board of estimate approved the contracts.

The Public Service Commission immediately notified the contractors to whom the awards had been made in May, 1908, to execute their contracts within the ten days allowed by contract provisions. All contractors signed their contracts within the time limit, and on November 9, 1909, the Commission formally approved and executed the same on behalf of the city. The contract for the first section in Flatbush Avenue extension was assigned, with the consent of the Commission, by James P. Graham to Smith, Scott and Company, who performed the work.

CONSTRUCTION BEGUN IN 1909

The first work on the subway was done on November 13, 1909, upon one of the sections for which William Bradley was the contractor. The first shovelful of earth was turned by William R. Willcox, then chairman of the Public Service Commission, in the presence of several thousand people. The occasion was made memorable by appropriate ceremonies carried out by a Brooklyn citizens committee. The place where this work was done was In Flatbush Avenue extension between DeKalb avenue and Willoughby street. .

Shortly after the contracts were awarded the Commission began negotiations which ended March 19, 1913, in the execution of the dual system contracts. Under one of these contracts the New York Municipal Railway Corporation was given a lease of the Fourth Avenue subway, its extensions and connections, for forty-nine years upon the terms and conditions laid down in contract No. 4.

In 1912, during the dual system negotiations, the Conference Committee of the Commission and the board of estimate and apportionment recommended the construction of the extension of the Fourth Avenue subway to 86th street as a part of the dual system. On February 15, 1912, this recommendation was approved by the board of estimate and apportionment, and on June 14, 1912, the Commission directed its chief engineer and counsel to prepare plans and contracts for such extension. After public advertising, the Commission on September 16, 1912, awarded the contracts for the construction of the extension (sections Nos. 1 and 2 of route No. 11-B) to the Degnon Contracting Company, the lowest bidder for each section. The contracts were delivered October 4, 1912, and the time limit for completion was two years from that date. The work was delayed by various causes, and the Commission upon application of the contractor has granted an extension of time fer section No. 1, extending from 43rd to 61st street, to July 1, 1915, and for section No. 2, extending from 61st to 86th street, to July 4, 1915. The contractor has completed two tracks as far as 65th street. where the connection is made with the reconstructed Sea Beach railroad.

PLANS MADE BY OLD COMMISSION

Plans for the Fourth Avenue subway were partially made by the engineering department of the Board of Rapid Transit Railroad Commissioners when George S. Rice was chief engineer of that board. It is a coincidence that Mr. Rice, who started this work ten years ago, is now division engineer for the Public

Service Commission in charge of the sixth division, which embraces the Fourth Avenue subway. The plans were drawn under Mr. Rice's direction by Sverre Dahm, then with the Rapid Transit Commission, and now principal assistant engineer in charge of the division of designs of the Public Service Commission. The actual drafting was in charge of Ralph Cranmer and Aaron I. Raisman, designing engineers, who also continued their work under the Public Service Commission. Mr. Cranmer died and was succeeded by Mr. Allen. The latter also died in service and was succeeded by Charles Rodenburg being at present designing engineer of the Public Service Commission. Charles E. Conover, designing engineer, and many others of the Commission's staff have since been engaged on this work.

After the Public Service Commission was organized the plans were redrawn practically by the same force under Henry B. Seaman, then chief engineer of the Commission, and the contracts awarded. It was upon Mr. Seaman's recommendation that the big bore subway was decided upon by the Commission. In 1911 Mr. Seaman resigned and Alfred Craven, the present incumbent, was made chief engineer. Under Mr. Craven the plans for the extension from 43rd street to 86th street were prepared and the contracts awarded.

ROUTE OF THE SUBWAY

From the Manhattan bridge, which crosses the East river at Canal street, Manhattan, the Fourth Avenue subway extends through Brooklyn and South Brooklyn to Fourth avenue and 86th street, which is within ten blocks of Fort Hamilton. Its trunk line contains four tracks (in places as many as six). The four tracks will enter Manhattan over the Manhattan bridge. Two of them, on the Manhattan side, connect with the two easterly tracks in the Centre street Loop subway. The other two continue under Canal street to a connection with the new subway running up Broadway. For temporary operation the loop tracks alone will be used, and trains bound for South Brooklyn will leave Manhattan from the Chambers Street station of that subway, in the basement of the new municipal building. The other two tracks will not be used until the Broadway subway is ready for operation. The route of the trunk line is as follows: From the Manhattan bridge under Flatbush Avenue extension, Fulton street, Ashland place and Fourth avenue to 86th street. The four-track construction extends from the bridge to about 84th street, where two tracks will connect with the reconstructed Sea Beach railroad of the New York Municipal Railway Corporation, and two tracks will continue under the westerly side of Fourth avenue to 86th street. The Sea Beach railroad has been rebuilt as a four-track line from Fourth avenue to Coney Island. The two local tracks will be used for temporary operation in connection with the Fourth Avenue subway, so that through trains will run from the municipal building in Manhattan to the Sea Beach terminal at Coney Island. The temporary operation will be a combination of local and express service. The local tracks will be used from the Manhattan bridge to 36th street and the express tracks from 36th to 64th street, where again the local tracks of the Sea Beach road will be utilized.

The Sea Beach line is owned by the railroad company, but is to be operated under the dual system contracts in connection with the Fourth Avenue subway, owned by the city of New York.

With the completion of the Whitehall-Montague Street tunnel under the East river, now in course of construction, the Fourth Avenue subway will have another connection with Manhattan. This tunnel will connect with the Fourth Avenue line in Flatbush Avenue extension just west of the DeKalb Avenue station.

With four tracks over the Manhattan bridge and two tracks through the tunnel, the Fourth Avenue subway will have access to Manhattan by six tracks. They will all be needed, however, for the Brighton Beach railroad and two new elevated railroads to Coney Island eventually will be connected with the Fourth Avenue subway and trains from all three lines operated through it. The Brighton Beach connection will be made by building a two-track subway, leaving the Fourth Avenue subway in Fulton street near Ashland place and extending through St. Felix street and Flatbush avenue to the Brighton Beach line at Malbone street. Construction work on a part of this line is already under way. It will be completed in about two years.

The two elevated lines to Coney Island will diverge from the Fourth Avenue subway at 38th street by means of two tracks and run thence by subway and open cut through the right of way of the company along 38th street to Tenth avenue, the city having purchased a perpetual easement through this right of way. West of the Ninth Avenue station these two tracks widen out into six tracks, which are carried three each on two levels. The upper tracks connect with the elevated structure which begins at Tenth avenue and runs down New Utrecht avenue, 86th street and Stillwell avenue to Coney Island. The tracks on the lower level swing to the north and, crossing Tenth avenue at 37th street, ascend until they join the elevated structure which runs parallel to 37th street to Gravesend avenue, thence continuing over the elevated structure down Gravesend avenue to Shell road, thence over Shell road to Coney Island.

The steel structure for the greater part of the New Utrecht Avenue line has been erected and it is expected this line will be ready for operation within a year. The completion of the Gravesend Avenue line may be looked for about six months later. No steel has yet been erected on this line, as the first contract was awarded only a few weeks ago.

CARS WILL BE LARGER THAN THOSE IN FIRST SUBWAY

Operation will begin with eight-car trains, made up of the new all-steel cars purchased by the New York Municipal Railway Corporation for dual system use. These cars are ten feet wide, one foot wider than the cars used in the existing subway. They are 67 feet long, or 16 feet longer than the existing subway cars. They will seat 78 passengers non-rush hours, against 44 and 46, respectively, in the present subway cars.

The company states that the rush-hour load in the existing subway is approximately 1,200 passengers per train of ten cars, or 440 passengers seated and 760 standing. An eight-car train of the new Brooklyn cars will carry the same load of 1,200 passengers, but will accommodate 624 seated passengers and 576 standing. It is also claimed that the standing passengers in the new cars will have a floor space averaging about five square feet per person as against an average of about two and a half square feet on the old subway cars.

CONSTRUCTION OF THE LINE

The Fourth Avenue subway, when completed, will have cost the city of New York about $30,000,000. The system will comprise about twenty miles of underground and elevated railroad and more than sixty-four miles of single track line.

Under the dual system contracts, the installation of the third-rail, the signal system, electric cables, cars, etc., are made a part of the equipment, which is to be supplied by the operating company at its own expense. The company has purchased 200 all-steel cars and awarded contracts for the installation of the signal system, the third-rail and other required track accessories.

The cost of real estate in addition to the construction price of the Fourth Avenue subway will be about $6,000,000. Up to June 1, 1915, the total expenditures by the city for real estate for this line were $208,310.58.

The total excavation was 2,487,901 cubic yards; the total concrete laid 464,039 cubic yards, and the total of steel work erected and placed 51,967 tons.

NEW FEATURES IN FOURTH AVENUE SUBWAY

In planning the Fourth Avenue subway, as well as the other new lines of the dual system, the engineers of the Public Service Commission departed in some respects from the plan of construction used in the first subway. In the original subway the height of the roof above the base of the rail is 12 feet 10 inches, and a width of about 12 feet 6 inches was allowed for each track. In the Fourth Avenue and Centre Street subways the height is 15 feet above the base of the rail and a width of 14 feet for each track is allowed.

This will make possible the operation of larger cars than those used in the first subway. The Brooklyn company, as before stated, has taken advantage of the increased dimensions to order a wider and more commodious car. In the matter of cooling and ventilating the underground structure, the Fourth

Avenue subway is expected to be superior to the older line. In the first subway extra precautions were taken to keep out water, and water proofing was placed under the floor, along the sides and over the roof of the tunnel. Experience has shown that while this waterproofing keeps out water it also prevents the heat from escaping as rapidly as it could if the walls were more porous. In the new structure waterproofing was used only in places where it was absolutely necessary to keep out water. As a result, it is expected that the Fourth Avenue road will be cooler in hot weather than the original subway was when placed in operation.

In ventilation the new structure is also expected to show improvement. The original subway was built as one large tunnel. On the trunk line, that is, between Brooklyn Bridge and 96th street, all four tracks run side by side in the same subway except for a stretch immediately south of 42nd street, where the northbound and southbound tracks pass through separate tunnels. In the Fourth Avenue and Centre Street Loop subways each track occupies a separate tunnel; that is, there are partitions between the tracks. In the original subway the lack of such partitions prevented the full utilization of the train movements to promote ventilation. While the frequent passage of trains in both directions stirred up the air, it did not entirely renew it and in consequence the city was put to additional expense to provide ventilating devices. In the new structure it is expected that the passage of trains will produce a piston action, driving the air out ahead of them and causing an inrush of fresh air by suction from the rear. In order to safeguard employees frequent archways are cut into the partition walls to provide places of refuge for track laborers. Fresh air is admitted by frequent openings in the roof of the subway, which are covered with gratings, and also through the openings at station entrances.

Another improvement which will be observed in the Fourth Avenue subway is that all of the station platforms will be straight, thus avoiding the danger and inconvenience of loading and unloading trains at stations having curved platforms. All express stations in the new subway are 480 feet long and local stations 435 feet long. These platforms will accommodate 8-car express trains and 6-car local trains of the large type, which will be used for Fourth Avenue operation.

In the construction of stations and station platforms several departures have been made from the plans used in the original subway. Booths for news stands are constructed as part of the subway walls and open upon the station platforms through windows. This adds to the fireproof character of the structure, by making unnecessary the installation of wooden stands, etc. Another advantage is that this arrangement prevents encumbering the platforms with news stands, and thereby makes available the maximum platform space.

The stations are finished in marble and white tile and each station has a separate color scheme. Different colored marbles are used for different stations, so that the passenger using the line every day will soon become accustomed to the color variation and will be able to identify a station by the shade of its marble trimmings. For instance, in the Gold Street station the marble and mosaic work are in yellow; the DeKalb Avenue station red; the Pacific Street station green; the Union Street station another shade of green; the 9th Street station rose color; the Prospect Avenue station light green; the 25th Street station light red, etc.

CHANGES IN ORIGINAL PLANS

Under the dual system contracts it was necessary to adapt the Fourth Avenue subway for operation by the New York Municipal Railway Corporation in connection with the Centre Street Loop and Broadway subways, allotted to it for operation, and also in connection with the existing elevated railroads in Brooklyn, as a part of the new system. Certain changes in the completed structure were found to be necessary. For instance, one of the new lines to be built by the city for operation by this company is the Whitehall-Montague Street route, extending from the lower part of Manhattan under the East River and Montague and other streets in Brooklyn to a connection with the Fourth Avenue subway in Flatbush Avenue extension. This connection will he made just west of the DeKalb Avenue station. It was therefore advisable to change the construction of this station so as to permit express trains which will be operated through the Whitehall Montague Street line to stop at the station. To accomplish this it was necessary to construct crossovers between the express and local tracks of the Fourth Avenue subway at this point. This work is now being done.

Another change was made at Fourth avenue and 38th street at the request of the company and in accordance with the requirements of Contract No. 4. The original plan provided for a connection through 40th street, with the proposed elevated railroads down New Utrecht avenue and 86th street and Gravesend avenue to Coney Island. The connection was shifted to 38th street, and in consequence the completed structure of the Fourth Avenue subway at that point had to be correspondingly changed. This change necessitated a partial reconstruction of the 36th Street station. Plans for the same were perfected and the Commission amended the contract. The work is now practically completed.

When the Fourth Avenue subway was under construction it was found necessary to carry in it temporarily one of the sewers which was to be displaced by the construction of an extensive relief sewer system. Pending the construction of this relief system the temporary sewer was allowed to occupy the space provided in the subway structure for the easterly local track between Hanson place and Butler street. About the end of the year 1914 the relief sewer system was completed, and the Commission immediately prepared plans for the removal of the temporary sewer. The contract for this work was awarded last March and it is nearly done. What remains will not interfere with operation.

PROVIDING FOR TRACK WORK

Immediately after providing for the necessary structural changes, the Commission gave its attention to the matter of tracks for the new subway. Early in 1914 it advertised for bids for steel rails, ties and other track materials and purchased a sufficient quantity for the equipment of the whole Fourth Avenue subway. Following the letting of contracts for such materials, it advertised for bids and awarded the contract for the laying of the tracks from Manhattan bridge to 86th street, the contractor to use the materials purchased by the city. This work is now nearly done.

During the summer of 1914 the Commission also advertised for bids and awarded the contract for station finish of the six stations on the extension of the Fourth Avenue subway between 43rd and 86th streets. Work under this contract is in progress.

It was also necessary to change the plans for the extension of the Fourth Avenue subway so as to provide for the connection with the Sea Beach railroad between 64th and 65th streets. With these exceptions the subway was built according to the plans originally adopted by the Commission in 1908.

LEASE FOR OPERATION

Under the dual system contracts, signed March 19, 1913, the New York Municipal Railway Corporation, a company formed by the Brooklyn Rapid Transit interests, is given a lease of the Fourth Avenue subway and other municipally-owned lines for forty-nine years in consideration of a contribution by the company toward the cost of construction, the right to operate and the purchase and maintenance of the equipment for all lines at the company's expense. The company's contribution is $13,500,000. The forty-nine year period will run from January 1, 1917, or from whatever date the Commission fixes for the beginning of permanent operation. Special terms are provided for temporary operation, and the Commission has the right to declare any portion of the new lines ready for temporary operation as soon as they are completed. It is under these terms that the operation of the Fourth Avenue subway is undertaken this month. This temporary operation will continue until the Broadway subway and other parts of the dual system allotted to the Brooklyn company for operation are completed. The operating company of the Brooklyn system will be the New York Consolidated Railroad Company.

The contracts provide that the rate of fare for a continuous ride over any line in the system operated by the Brooklyn company shall be five cents. This system will include not only the city-owned subways but also all the elevated railroads operated by the Brooklyn company. The only exception to the five-cent rate is the fare between Manhattan and Coney Island, and this eventually will be reduced to five cents, but under the terms of the contract the company has the right to continue the present ten-cent fare until through train operation by the Fourth Avenue subway and over the new Utrecht Avenue and Gravesend

Avenue elevated branches is possible. Within a year, or at most, two years, therefore, the five-cent fare to Coney Island will be in force. Free transfers also will be given at all intersecting points. When the entire system is completed a passenger will be able to travel from the terminus of the Queens lines to and through Manhattan and through Brooklyn to Coney Island—a distance of twenty-six miles for a single five-cent fare.

The lease provides for an equal division of profits between the city and the company after certain deductions have been made from the revenues. The receipts from all lines covered by the operating contract will be pooled, and each quarter deductions are to be made therefrom to pay operating expenses, rentals, taxes, maintenance and depreciation. In addition a deduction equivalent to $3,500,000 a year is to be made and paid to the company as representing the average annual profits which it was receiving from the operation of its own lines, embraced in the dual system, for two years prior to the beginning of operation under the new contract. There are also to be deducted amounts sufficient to pay interest upon the capital invested by the company in construction and equipment and by the city in construction. The amount remaining after these deductions are made is to be divided equally between the city and the company. Temporary operation will be conducted upon similar terms, the pooling of earnings taking place as soon as a new line is placed in operation. In the case of the New York Municipal Railway Corporation such operation began August 3, 1913, when the Centre Street Loop subway was opened for traffic.

Speaking of New Cars

We Are Actually Building Them; Not Merely Talking About It.

THE OTHER DAY a Brooklyn member of the Legislative Committee which is conducting one of the many pending investigations of the rapid transit situation, was quoted in a newspaper account of the Committee's hearings, as saying, when advised that we expected to operate our trains into Queens under the Dual System Contracts:

"That's news to me."

Perhaps it will be news to some of our readers that a substantial number of our new steel subway cars (part of a lot of 200 now ordered and in the course of construction as a starter on the eventual supply of 600 of these cars) are now complete and will soon be in experimental operation on the Sea Beach line.

It may even be news to some that the Sea Beach line, built as a four-track depressed rapid transit railroad, is practically finished after about a year and a half of construction work, and will be waiting several months for the completion of the seven year job on the Fourth Avenue subway before it can give to South Brooklyn the relief so long promised.

SUBWAY CAR EXTERIOR

These new steel subway cars, more of which are approaching completion weekly, are quite interesting things in themselves.

They are, to begin with, 67 feet long and ten feet wide. The present New York subway cars are 51 feet long and eight and one-half feet wide.

It has sometimes been suggested to us by those in positions of municipal authority, that we should reduce the size of our cars to the standard of the Interborough's equipment, so that if we ever merged with the Interborough, or the Interborough merged with us, or the city took over both systems, the car equipment could be interchangeably operated on all lines.

We have always replied to these suggestions that we never knew any one to make progress by moving backwards.

We have also remarked that after the city had spent tens of millions in building its new subways bigger than its old ones, so as to give better accommodations to its people, we, at least, did not propose to become a party to a waste of this expenditure.

So our new cars have remained 67 feet long and ten feet wide (just the right size for the new subways) despite all efforts to shrink them.

Our new subway cars will seat 78 persons with all doors in operation. The present Interborough subway cars seat 44 persons under similar conditions.

The present evening rush hour subway load at Brooklyn Bridge, northbound, is said to be about 1200 persons per train. A ten car Interborough train will therefore have 440 people sitting and 760 standing, and as there are about 1870 square feet of floor space inside the

INTERIOR OF SUBWAY CAR

EIGHT CAR TRAIN, N. Y. MUNICIPAL RAILWAY

ten cars, the standing passengers have approximately 2½ square feet each—a space 24 inches by 15 inches.

If an eight car train of our new cars is obliged to carry a similar rush hour load, it will seat 624 passengers, have 576 passengers standing, and allow four and a half square feet of floor space for each standing passenger.

If any of our readers wishes to assume, in an effort to obtain as gloomy a view of the future as possible, that notwithstanding all the new transit routes, rush hour trains after all the new lines are done, will have to carry as many people as they do now, we suggest that a little cheer can be obtained by measuring out a space 24 inches by 27 inches (four and a half square feet) and then seeing whether it is possible to stand therein without being unpleasantly jostled by one's neighbors occupying similar spaces.

In the non-rush hours, our new subway cars will seat 90 persons, when only a single set of doors is operated.

There are three pairs of doors on each side. The average walk for all passengers from seat to door is only six feet, ten and one-half inches—a little over two paces.

The streams of passengers entering and leaving the cars are broken up and guided to the seating area tributary to each set of doors. Thus the possibility of a jam in one part of a car, though there may be plenty of room somewhere else, is largely done away with.

The seats are built from plans developed through co-operation between our engineers and the American Posture League, an association of orthopedic specialists working disinterestedly for the public health. The seat design holds the body in a comfortable and correct position, and makes a bad posture possible only through a conscious contortion to avoid fitting into the seat cushions.

There are no straps in these cars. White enameled posts in groups of four at each set of doors will keep the standing load (which will never be escaped in rush hours if New York City keeps on growing) nearest the exits, so that the doors will clear automatically before most of the seated passengers have a chance to reach them.

The new subway cars are, of course, of steel construction throughout.

The interior decoration, largely white enamel, was developed in connection with a scientific study of the lighting problem. Sanitary floor corners render impossible the accumulation of dirt and reduce to a minimum the opportunities for germs to gather and breed.

An emergency lighting system, independent of outside power supply, will, if operating current is cut off, turn on emergency lights automatically throughout the train.

The doors are equipped with a pneumatic cushion, so that one may, if he chooses, deliberately allow a door to close on his arm or other part of his body without injury. All doors are operated by an electro-pneumatic device giving a higher degree of control than anything previously used in railroad operation.

The starting signals are so interlocked with the doors that the signal to start the train cannot show in the motorman's cab until every door on the train is closed.

An automatic speed control system makes it impossible for a train of these cars to exceed a predetermined speed when going down grades.

In every car there is an emergency valve which, if pulled by the conductor, will shut off the power and apply the emergency brakes throughout the train.

So we might go on at even greater length, but, for the purposes of this pamphlet, we think the pictures we have produced tell a better story than any number of words.

We are proud of our new subway car. We think Brooklyn will be proud of it when it is carrying Brooklyn up Broadway in Manhattan.

We are telling a little something about the car at this time, because it is at times a good plan to look ahead, as well as behind us, or directly at the patch of ground on which we may be standing just at the present moment.

BROOKLYN RAPID TRANSIT COMPANY.

February 9, 1915.

October-November 1914

38th Street looking North on 4th Avenue

38th Street and 4th Avenue Bridge looking West

Stiff-Legged Derrick

Interior of Machine Shop

Photo No. 67. Route 39. Sec. No. 1. N. Y. Munic. R'y Corp. Plant—1-yard Lakewood Concrete Mixer with Tower. Oct. 28, 1914

Interior of Machine Shop

Portable motor-driven compressor

High Air Double Phase Compressor

Lakewood Concrete Mixer

Stiff-Legged Traveller Derrick

Portable Stiff-Legged Derrick

Photo No. 82. Route 39. Sec. No. 1. N. Y. Munic. R'y Corp. Plant---Showing motor driven direct connected centrifugal pump. Nov. 9, 1914

Motor-driven direct connected centrifugal pump

Small Lakewood concrete mixer

Motor driven gear connected compressor in operation

Section of the incline to the Fifth Avenue Elevated in place. Looking South.

36th Street station remodelling. Showing wall removal of old bellmouth. West Side. Looking North.

36th Street station remodelling. Showing wall removal. West Side. Looking North.

Photo No. 89. Route 39. Sec. No. 1. N. Y. Munic. R'y Cor
Showing Underpinning Elevated Ry. Columns. Looking West
Oct. 24, 191

38th Street Extension. Showing channels for conduit line

38th Street extension. Interior of South Brooklyn Railway tunnel. Looking west.

Photo No. 100. Route 39. Sec No. 1. N. Y. Munic. R'y Corp. 36th St. Sta. Remodeling. Chipping invert, east side, for splice after wall removed. Looking North   Oct. 28, 1914

Underpinning elevated columns. Showing columns on new piers. Trusses removed.

Two kinds of sheathing hammers in action.

36th Street Station remodeling showing nitches made in concrete roof for new girders.

36th Street Station remodeling showing roof removal between 37th and 38th Streets looking North.

Photo No. 105. Route 39. Sec. No. 1. N. Y. Munic. R'y Corp. 36th St. Sta. Remodeling. Remodeling of steel in place. Showing a cut-off column that has been remodeled and a new girder placed thereon. Nov. 9, 1914

Photo No. 106. Route 39. Sec. No. 1. N. Y. Munic. R'y Corp.
Underpinning Elevated Columns. Showing new concrete pier from grillage underneath up.
Nov. 9, 1914

December 1914

Photo No. 118. Route 39. Sec. No. 1. N. Y. Munic. R'y Corp. 36th St. Station Remodeling. Remodeling Steel, showing old girders, new columns, and connections. Dec. 19, 1914

Photo No. 119. Route 39. Sec. No. 1. N. Y. Munic. R'y Corp
36th St. Station Remodeling. Steel Erection---Showing arrange
ment of floor beams and wall columns for incline tracks.
Dec. 18, 1914

36th Street Station remodeling. Floor beams with connections to old steel for incline tracks

36th Street Station remodeling. Showing completed section of steel erection and concreted invert for incline track

36th Street Station remodeling. Showing cutoff columns with connections for floor beams.

36th Street Station remodeling. Showing invert partly completed columns and girders in place, 34th Street looking Southeast

January 1915

36th Street Station remodeling. 33rd Street West Side. Looking Southwest. Showing west wall forms and new steel in place.

36th Street Station remodeling. Showing invert splice, new grillages at center and new steel. 35th St West

36th St. Station remodeling. Looking northeast at 35th St - east side. Showing excavation for invert and new outside wall.

36th St. Station remodeling. Looking south and showing new side walls, roof and beginning of west incline.

37th Street west side looking south. Showing new concrete invert and steel in place for west incline.

37th Street East side, looking North.

Photo No. 134. Route 39. Sec. No. 1. N. Y. Munic. R'y Co
36th St. Station Remodelling. 37th St. East side. Looking W.
Showing new West incline and steel remodelling for East incl

37th and 38th Streets west side, looking north. Showing remodeling of old steel and new steel for East incline

Reconstruction for new portal to west incline and crossover. Looking Northwest.

Recontruction for new portal to east incline and crossover. Looking Northwest.

General view of new portal to two incline tracks and north wall of 38th Street cut. Looking Northeast.

General view of new portals to two incline tracks. Looking Northwest.

38th Street Extension. Showing steel in place for conduct platform and grading for final track in old South Brooklyn Railway brick tunnel.

38th Street Extension. Showing old south wall to be removed and Shovel No. 1 excavating for new north wall at 7th Avenue. Looking Northwest.

38th Street Extension. General view of 38th Street cut from 9th Avenue looking East. Shovel No. 2 excavating for new South wall.

March 1915

38th Street Extension. General view of 38th Street cut from 9th Avenue looking West.

38th Street Extension. General view of 38th Street cut from Ninth Avenue looking East.

36th Street Station remodeling. Showing new roof in place. Looking Northeast.

36th Street Station remodeling. Showing interior walls, invert, and roof in place. Looking South.

36th Street Station remodeling. Showing invert splice, new wall and roof ready for concrete. West Side looking South

36th Street Station remodeling. Showing forms with steel and reinforcing bars in place for one section of new platform. West side looking Southeast.

36th Street Station remodeling. General view of South Bound or West incline and crossover, looking North, showing curtain wall and roof concrete forms.

36th Street Station remodeling. Showing invert and walls under construction for the Northbound incline track. Looking Northwest.

36th Street Station remodeling. Showing reconstruction of Culver on Fourth Avenue Bridge over 38th Street. Looking East.

36th Street Station remodeling. Showing new portal under construction for 38th Street connection to Fourth Avenue Subway. Looking Northwest.

38th Street extension showing old South retaining wall before removal. Looking North

38th Street extension showing duct platform with some ducts in place in old South Brooklyn Railway brick tunnel

38th Street extension. General view of 38th Street reconstruction from portal of old tunnel. Looking East.

38th Street extension. General view of steel erection for South Brooklyn tunnel extension seen from above.

Preparations for underpinning Fifth Avenue Elevated column.

Old North wall of 38th Street cut before removal.

36th Street Station remodeling. Showing new roof steel for incline track and new steel connected to old steel. Looking East.

New roof of ascending track from the old South Mezzanine Floor of the 36th Street Station.

36th Street Station remodeling showing new roof steel connected to old.

36th Street Station remodeling - general view of reconstruction.

36th Street Station remodeling - showing the waterproofing of the new concrete roof.

38th Street extension showing the erection of steel for the South Brooklyn tunnel extension.

38th Street extension general view looking West showing the inclines, subway station and new south wall from between 7th and 8th Avenues.

General view of the site for the 9th Avenue Station. Looking Northwest.

Concrete grillages for the Ninth Avenue Station. Looking West.

General view of the site for the 9th Avenue Station. Looking Northeast

Roof steel for extension to South Brooklyn Railway tunnel.

Underpinning the elevated railway columns for the 38th Street extension.

Underpinning of the elevated railway columns and removal of the North Wall. Looking North.

April 1915

General interior view of new construction: 36th Street Station remodeling.

New Platforms in place on east side of the 36th Street Station

36th Street Station showing connection with new steel construction and old.

View of the new chamber for descending track.

South Brooklyn Railway Co old brick tunnel showing new conduit platform in place and new track under construction

May 1915

General view of Ninth Avenue Station showing covered and uncovered portions. Looking Southwest.

General view of the Ninth Avenue Station from near Ninth Avenue. Looking Northwest.

East end of Ninth Avenue Station showing both levels. Looking Northwest.

Area East of Ninth Avenue Station Looking towards Tenth Ave and 37th St.

Ninth Avenue Station lower level under construction. Looking East.

Compartment for telephone and signal apparatus in manhole at 33rd Street on West side.

View of north bank of Culver deviation showing boulders encountered during shovel excavation.

Fifth Avenue Elevated incline, new South retaining walls and portal of new extension.

General view of south bank of the 38th St extension, between Seventh and Eighth Avenues

View from north bank between Seventh and Eighth Avenues

View from north bank between Eighth and Ninth Avenues showing new walls and yard approach.

June 1915

Retaining wall section showing roof of yard approach platform from North side looking Northwest.

View of retaining wall section showing approaches for Ninth Avenue Station taken from North bank west of Ninth Avenue. Looking Northwest.

38th Street extension showing Type II track assembled and ready for concrete at the lower level of the Ninth Avenue Station

Upper level platform and canopies of the Ninth Avenue Station from South side East of Ninth Avenue. Looking Northwest.

Area excavated for Sub-Section No. 10. Looking West from near Tenth Avenue.

Forms for footings of Sub-Section No. 10. Taken from East portal of Ninth Avenue Station.

Construction of Sub-Section No.10 from south bank east of Ninth Avenue Station.

Walls of West End approach and backfilling.

July 1915

General view of retaining wall section showing portal at station and inclines taken from roof of yard approach platform.

General view of 38th Street cut showing portal of Ninth Avenue Station in distance taken from roof of yard approach incline. Looking East.

General view of retaining wall section showing yard approach platform inclines and portal at station. Looking West.

General view of Ninth Avenue Station from south bank east of Ninth Avenue. Looking northwest.

View of West end of Ninth Avenue Station upper level looking East.

General view showing West End approch.

General view showing portal of Sub Section No. 10. Looking Southwest.

August 1915

General view looking West from West End approach showing upper level of Sub Section No.10 and Ninth Avenue Station.

General view looking East from Ninth Avenue.

General view looking West from Ninth Avenue.

General view of retaining wall section looking West showing yard approach and Fifth Avenue Elevated inclines.

General view of retaining wall section looking East from portal of yard approach platform.

General view looking East from Culver Line showing cut for new Culver deviation.

Circuit breaker chamber on North side of old brick tunnel.

General view of Type II track concreted.

Looking East from Ninth Avenue.

Ninth Avenue Station building on roof of upper level.

New Westbound Culver deviation track.

Shovel No. 1 working in the 36th Street Yard.

View of Type II track assembled.

View of Type II track lined up

View of Type II track suspended and ready for concreting.

View of Type II track being concreted.

September 1915

Excavation of prism between Culver deviation tracks and 38th Street cut looking East.

Excavation of prism between Culver deviation tracks and 38th Street cut looking West.

Ninth Avenue Station building looking Southeast.

Ninth Avenue Station building looking Northeast.

South slope looking West from West End Bridge.

General view of Ninth Avenue Station looking West.

85

38th Street prism excavation showing boulders encountered.

Tenth Avenue open cut section.

Sub Section No. 10 looking West from portal.

Ninth Avenue Station building looking Southeast.

Ninth Avenue Station building looking Northeast.

Type I track North half Special portion No. 31

Type I track South half Special Portion No. 31

Type I track Special Portion No. 30.

Type I track Special Portion No. 29

Type I track Special Portion No. 28

Type I track Special Portion No. 27 looking East.

CULVER EXP.
CULVER L'C'L.
WEST END EXP.
WEST END L'C'L

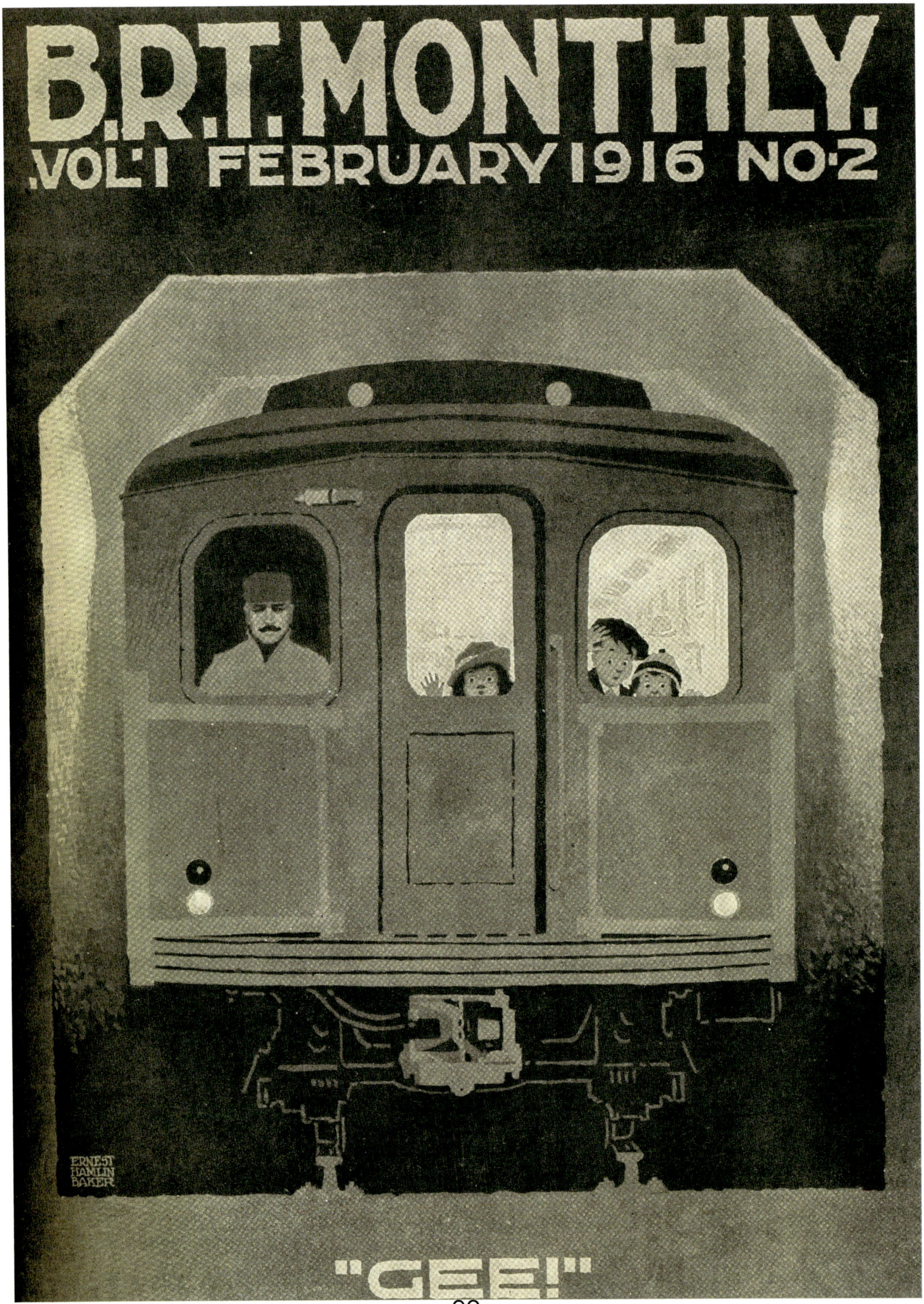
B.R.T. MONTHLY.
VOL. 1 FEBRUARY 1916 NO. 2
ERNEST HAMLIN BAKER
"GEE!"

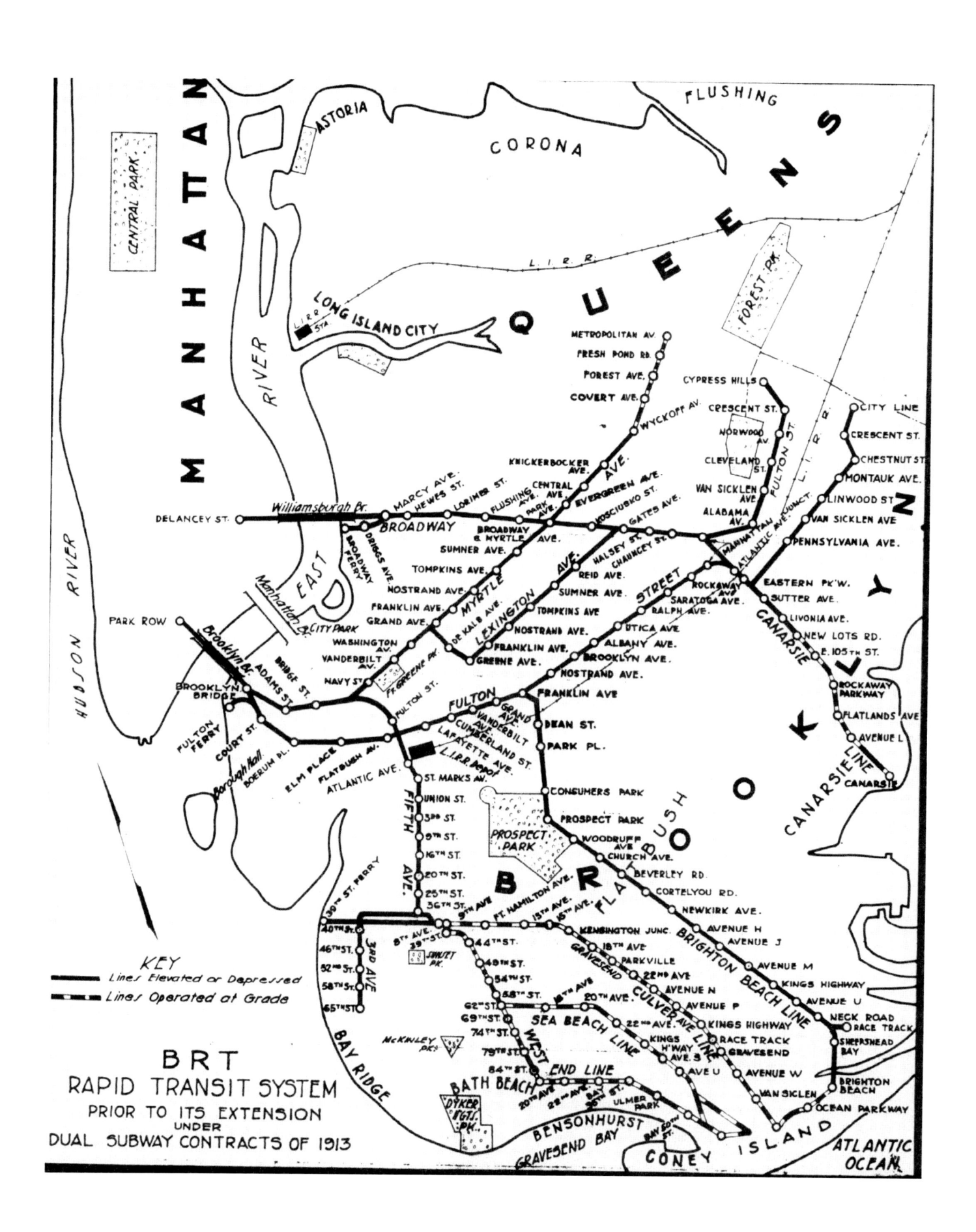

BRT RAPID TRANSIT SYSTEM PRIOR TO ITS EXTENSION UNDER DUAL SUBWAY CONTRACTS OF 1913

TRI-BOROUGH RAPID TRANSIT RAILROAD.

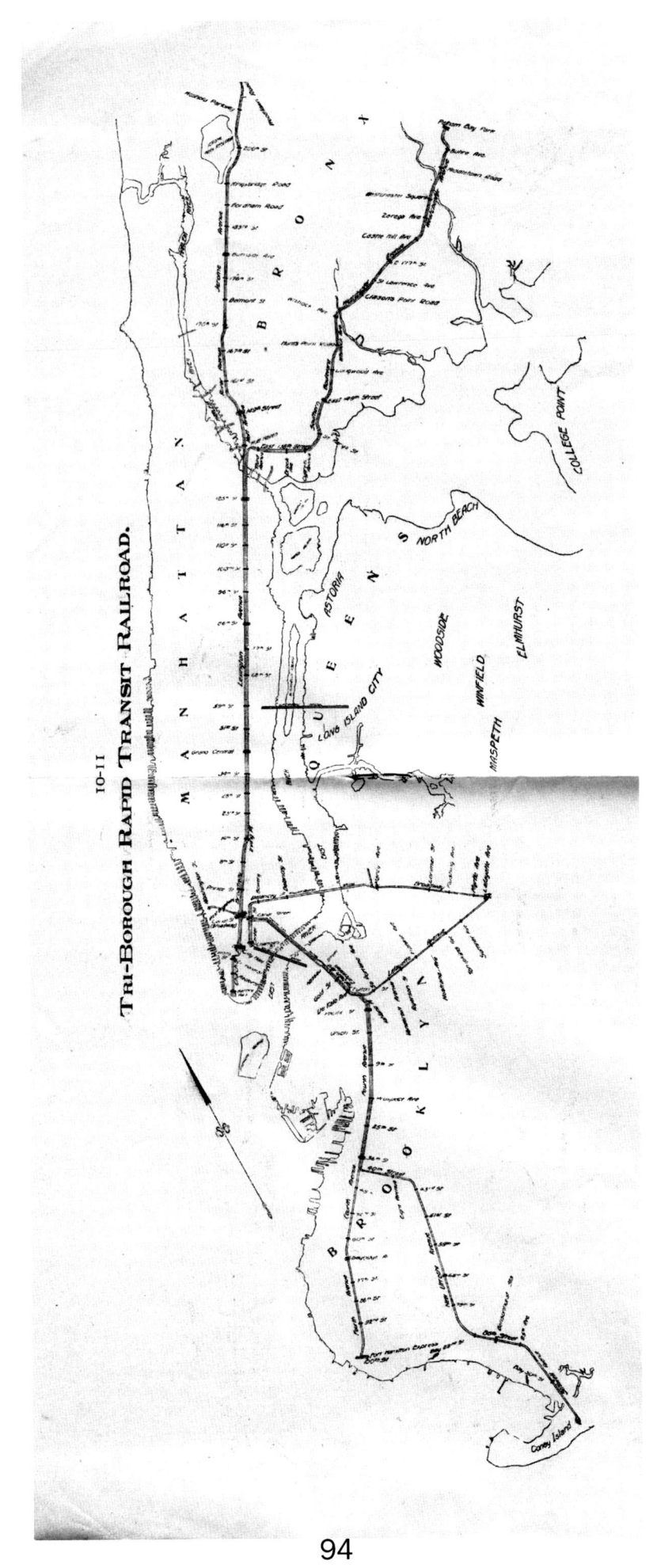

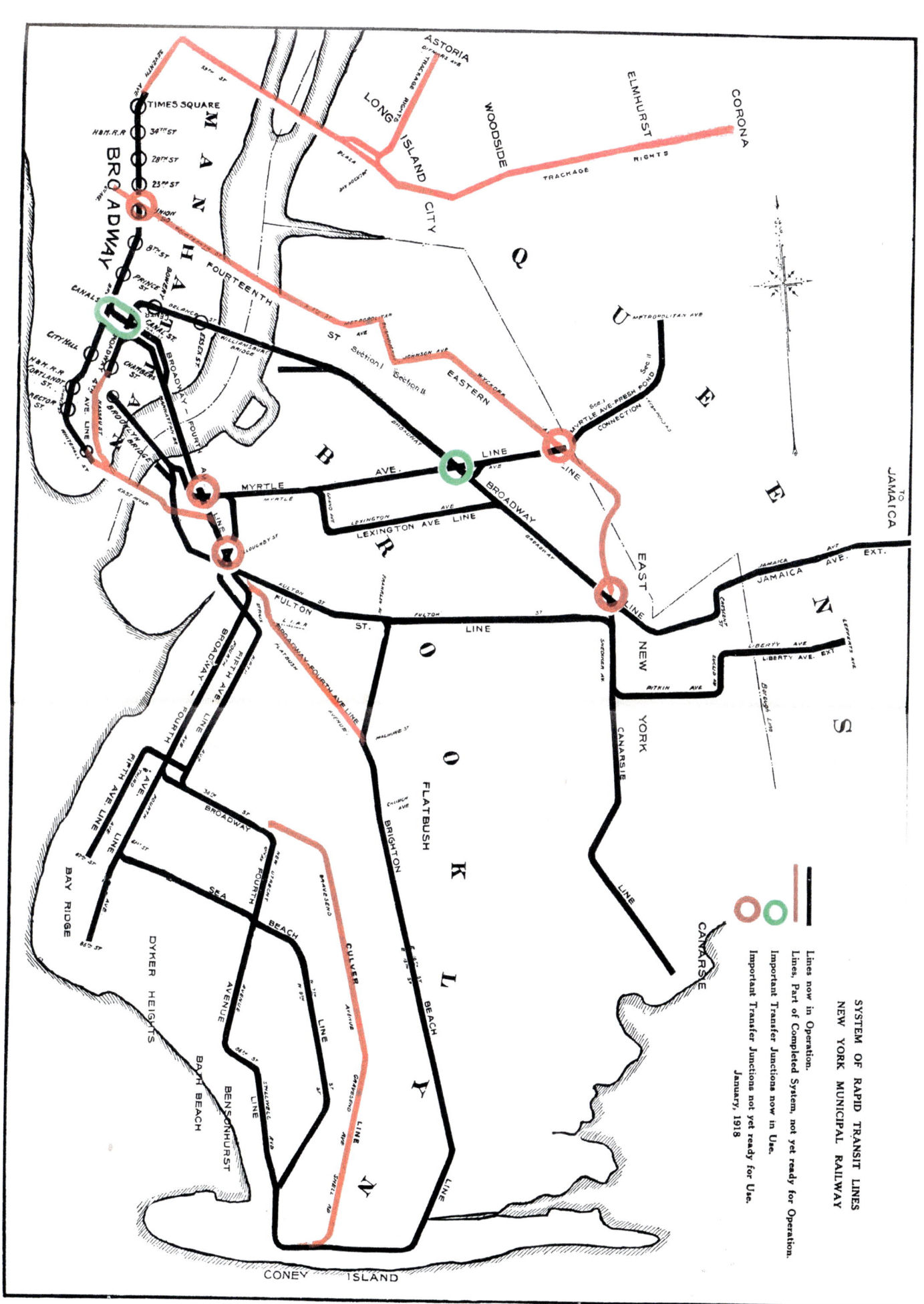

SYSTEM OF RAPID TRANSIT LINES
NEW YORK MUNICIPAL RAILWAY
January, 1918

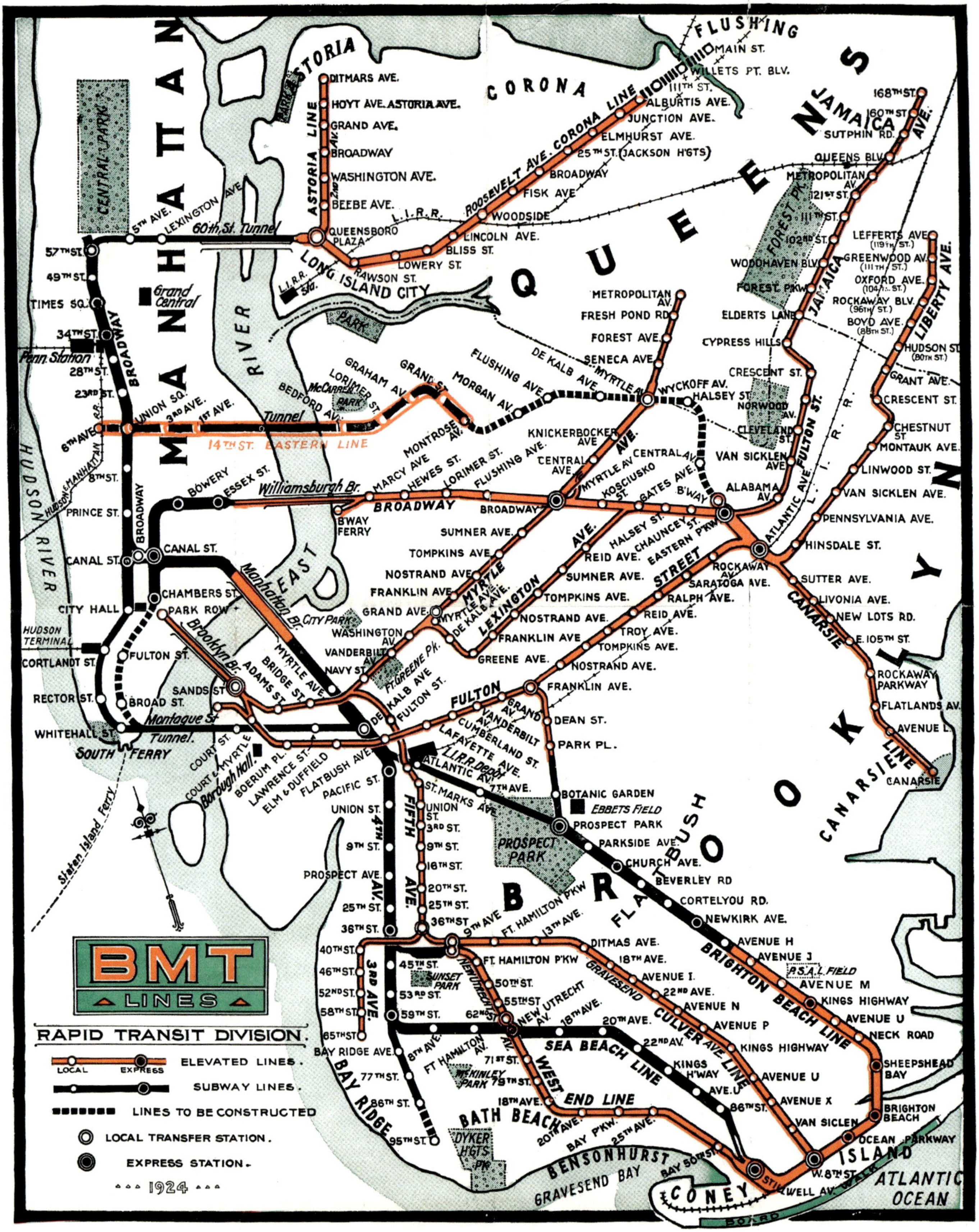
BMT
LINES
RAPID TRANSIT DIVISION.
LOCAL
EXPRESS
ELEVATED LINES.
SUBWAY LINES.
LINES TO BE CONSTRUCTED
LOCAL TRANSFER STATION.
EXPRESS STATION.
1924
MANHATTAN
QUEENS
BROOKLYN
ASTORIA
CORONA
FLUSHING
JAMAICA
LONG ISLAND CITY
CENTRAL PARK
HUDSON RIVER
EAST RIVER
ATLANTIC OCEAN
GRAVESEND BAY
CONEY ISLAND
BENSONHURST
BATH BEACH
BAY RIDGE
PROSPECT PARK
FOREST PK.
DYKER HGTS PK
SUNSET PARK
McKINLEY PARK
CITY PARK
FT. GREENE PK.
McCARREN PARK
EBBETS FIELD
P.S.A.L. FIELD
Grand Central
Penn Station
HUDSON TERMINAL
L.I.R.R.
L.I.R.R. Depot
Staten Island Ferry
60th St. Tunnel
14TH ST. EASTERN LINE
Tunnel
Williamsburgh Br.
Manhattan Br.
Brooklyn Br.
Montague St Tunnel.
Borough Hall
SOUTH FERRY
ASTORIA LINE
ROOSEVELT AVE. CORONA LINE
BROADWAY
MYRTLE AVE.
LEXINGTON AVE.
FULTON STREET
FULTON ST.
CANARSIE LINE
LIBERTY AVE.
JAMAICA AVE.
FIFTH AVE.
4TH AV.
3RD AVE.
SEA BEACH LINE
WEST END LINE
CULVER AVE. LINE
BRIGHTON BEACH LINE
FLATBUSH
GRAVESEND
NEW UTRECHT
DITMARS AVE.
HOYT AVE. ASTORIA AVE.
GRAND AVE.
BROADWAY
WASHINGTON AVE.
BEEBE AVE.
QUEENSBORO PLAZA
RAWSON ST.
LOWERY ST.
BLISS ST.
LINCOLN AVE.
WOODSIDE
FISK AVE.
25TH ST. (JACKSON H'GTS)
ELMHURST AVE.
JUNCTION AVE.
ALBURTIS AVE.
111TH ST.
WILLETS PT. BLV.
MAIN ST.
57TH ST.
49TH ST.
TIMES SQ.
34TH ST.
28TH ST.
23RD ST.
UNION SQ.
8TH ST.
PRINCE ST.
CANAL ST.
CITY HALL
CORTLANDT ST.
RECTOR ST.
WHITEHALL ST.
5TH AVE.
LEXINGTON AVE.
6TH AVE.
3RD AVE.
1ST AVE.
BOWERY
ESSEX ST.
CANAL ST.
CHAMBERS ST.
PARK ROW
FULTON ST.
BROAD ST.
SANDS ST.
ADAMS ST.
BRIDGE ST.
MYRTLE AVE.
DE KALB AVE
COURT ST.
COURT & MYRTLE
BOERUM PL.
LAWRENCE ST.
ELM & DUFFIELD
FLATBUSH AVE.
PACIFIC ST.
UNION ST.
9TH ST.
PROSPECT AVE.
25TH ST.
36TH ST.
40TH ST.
46TH ST.
52ND ST.
58TH ST.
65TH ST.
BAY RIDGE AVE.
45TH ST.
53RD ST.
59TH ST.
8TH AVE.
77TH ST.
86TH ST.
95TH ST.
ATLANTIC AV.
ST. MARKS AVE.
UNION ST.
3RD ST.
9TH ST.
16TH ST.
20TH ST.
25TH ST.
36TH ST.
9TH AVE.
FT. HAMILTON P'KW
13TH AVE.
50TH ST.
55TH ST.
62ND ST.
71ST ST.
79TH ST.
18TH AVE.
20TH AVE.
BAY P'KW.
25TH AVE.
BAY 50TH ST.
18TH AVE.
20TH AVE.
22ND AV.
KINGS H'WAY
AVE. U
86TH ST.
DITMAS AVE.
18TH AVE.
AVENUE I.
22ND AVE.
AVENUE N
AVENUE P
KINGS HIGHWAY
AVENUE U
AVENUE X
VAN SICLEN
W. 8TH ST.
STILLWELL AV.
OCEAN PARKWAY
BRIGHTON BEACH
SHEEPSHEAD BAY
NECK ROAD
AVENUE U
KINGS HIGHWAY
AVENUE M
AVENUE J
AVENUE H
NEWKIRK AVE.
CORTELYOU RD.
BEVERLEY RD
CHURCH AVE.
PARKSIDE AVE.
PROSPECT PARK
BOTANIC GARDEN
7TH AVE.
LAFAYETTE AVE.
CUMBERLAND ST.
VANDERBILT AV.
GRAND AV.
DEAN ST.
PARK PL.
FRANKLIN AVE.
NOSTRAND AVE.
TOMPKINS AVE.
TROY AVE.
REID AVE.
RALPH AVE.
SARATOGA AVE.
ROCKAWAY AV.
GREENE AVE.
FRANKLIN AVE
NOSTRAND AVE.
TOMPKINS AVE.
SUMNER AVE.
REID AVE.
HALSEY ST.
CHAUNCEY ST.
EASTERN P'KW
WASHINGTON AV.
VANDERBILT AV.
NAVY ST.
GRAND AVE.
MYRTLE AVE.
DE KALB AVE.
FRANKLIN AVE.
NOSTRAND AVE.
TOMPKINS AVE.
SUMNER AVE.
B'WAY FERRY
MARCY AVE
HEWES ST.
LORIMER ST.
FLUSHING AVE.
BROADWAY
MYRTLE AV.
KOSCIUSKO ST.
GATES AVE.
B'WAY
CENTRAL AVE.
KNICKERBOCKER AVE
CENTRAL AV.
MONTROSE AV.
BEDFORD AV.
LORIMER ST.
GRAHAM AV.
GRAND ST.
MORGAN AV.
FLUSHING AVE.
DE KALB AVE.
MYRTLE AV.
WYCKOFF AV.
HALSEY ST.
SENECA AVE.
FOREST AVE.
FRESH POND RD.
METROPOLITAN AV.
NORWOOD AV.
CLEVELAND ST.
VAN SICKLEN AVE
ALABAMA AV.
ATLANTIC AVE.
CRESCENT ST.
CYPRESS HILLS
ELDERTS LANE
FOREST PKW
WOODHAVEN BLV
102ND ST.
111TH ST.
121ST ST.
METROPOLITAN AV.
QUEENS BLV.
SUTPHIN RD.
160TH ST.
168TH ST.
LEFFERTS AVE (119TH ST.)
GREENWOOD AV. (111TH ST.)
OXFORD AVE. (104TH ST.)
ROCKAWAY BLV. (96TH ST.)
BOYD AVE. (88TH ST.)
HUDSON ST. (80TH ST.)
GRANT AVE.
CRESCENT ST.
CHESTNUT ST.
MONTAUK AVE.
LINWOOD ST.
VAN SICKLEN AVE.
PENNSYLVANIA AVE.
HINSDALE ST.
SUTTER AVE.
LIVONIA AVE.
NEW LOTS RD.
E. 105TH ST.
ROCKAWAY PARKWAY
FLATLANDS AV.
AVENUE L
CANARSIE

Advertisement

SUBWAY AL
THE WHISTLE AND ROLL SIGN STORE

www.SubwayAl.com

SUBWAYAL RAILROAD MEMORABILIA

SubwayAl offers a variety of antique transportation items, including original, mint copies of the famous 1972 New York Subway Map (by Massimo Vignelli), and an assortment of Vellum roll sign sections from retired New York Subway Cars.

CONTACT:
AZ@SUBWAYAL.COM

CULVER EXP.
CULVER L'C'L.
WEST END EXP.
WEST END L'C'L.
SEA BEACH EXP.
SEA BEACH L'C'L.
VIA BRIDGE
VIA TUNNEL
NASSAU ST.
BRIGHTON EXP.
BRIGHTON L'C'L.
FOURTH AV. L'C'L.
EXPRESS
LOCAL
MYRTLE AV. EXP.
MYRTLE AV. L'C'L.
BROADWAY B'KLYN. EXP.
BROADWAY B'KLYN. L'C'L.
JAMAICA EXP.
JAMAICA L'C'L.
14TH ST. L'C'L.
14TH ST. EXP.
14TH ST. LINE.

OTHER BOOKS BY THE AUTHOR

TRACKS OF THE INDEPENDENT SUBWAY
1937 - 1940

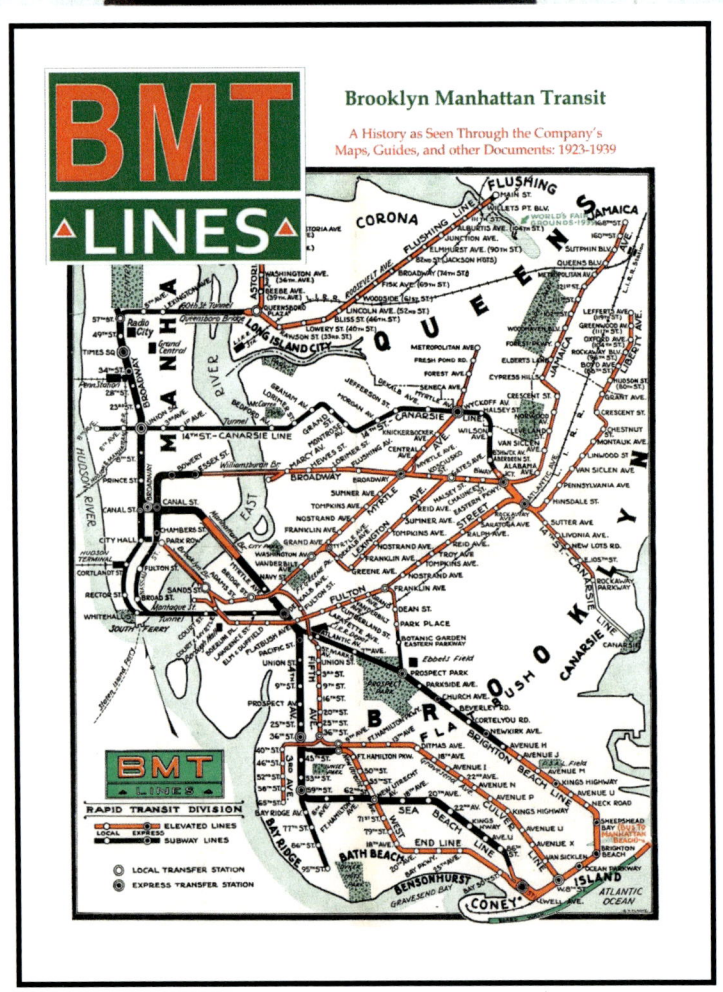

BMT LINES

Brooklyn Manhattan Transit

A History as Seen Through the Company's Maps, Guides, and other Documents: 1923-1939

Made in the USA
Middletown, DE
10 August 2019